panini

panini

Simple Recipes for Classic Italian Sandwiches

JENNIFER JOYCE   *photography by* **William Reavell**

LONDON • NEW YORK

Senior Designer **Paul Tilby**
Senior Editor **Julia Charles**
Production **Toby Marshall**
Publishing Director **Alison Starling**

Food Stylist **Gizzy Erskine**
Stylist **Helen Trent**
Indexer **Hilary Bird**

First published in the
United States in 2008
This edition published in 2012
by Ryland Peters & Small, Inc.
519 Broadway, 5th Floor
New York, NY 10012
www.rylandpeters.com

10 9 8 7 6 5 4 3 2

ISBN: 978 1 84975 309 8

The original edition of this book is cataloged as follows:
**Library of Congress Cataloging-in-Publication
Data**

Joyce, Jennifer.
  Panini : simple recipes for classic Italian sandwiches / Jennifer
Joyce ; photography by William Reavell.
    p. cm.
  Includes index.
  ISBN-13: 978-1-84597-608-8
  ISBN-10: 1-84597-608-8
  1. Sandwiches. 2 Çookery, Italian. I. Title.
TX818.J69 2008
641.8′4–dc22   2007025395

Printed in China

Notes

- All spoon measurements are level, unless otherwise specified.
- The recipes in this book have been written for use with a specially designed panini grill. If you do not have a panini grill you can still follow the recipes and prepare your panini using a skillet or ridged stovetop grill pan and a metal spatula. Simply preheat a skillet or grill pan over high heat, add the panini and cook for 2–3 minutes on each side, using the metal spatula to apply pressure.
- Ovens should be preheated to the specified temperature. Recipes in this book were tested using a regular oven. If using a fan-assisted oven, follow the manufacturer's instructions for adjusting temperature

Acknowledgments

We are grateful to Cuisinart® for providing the Panini and Sandwich Grill used to prepare the food photographed in this book. To find out more about their range of kitchen accessories and small appliances visit www.cuisinart.com

CONTENTS

Who but the Italians (with their love of simple, honest food) could have invented panini? The word means "little breads" but translates as warm, melting cheese and spicy salami or vegetables in a crisp jacket of warm bread. Although in Italy you find variations such as tramezzini or stuffed focaccia, this book focuses solely on simple, grilled panini—uncomplicated food at its finest.

To make these tasty bites there is one important prerequisite—buy the best ingredients you can find. Plunder your local market's deli counter and Italian stores for authentic cheeses such as Mozzarella, Fontina, or Provolone and delicious meats such as prosciutto, bresaola, and mortadella salami. The golden rule of sucessful panini making is not to overcomplicate things. Use no more than 4–5 fillings, including cheese, salami/meat, and grilled vegetables. Almost any fillings will work, but keep watery lettuces and mayonnaises on the side instead of inside your sandwich. Arugula and watercress are the exceptions as they retain their texture and spiciness after heating.

Ciabatta is best but you can use any good-quality bread. Brioche or sliced white, for instance, suits sweet panini, while ciabatta is best for savory panini. Partially baked ciabatta (sold at larger grocers) doesn't need time in the oven beforehand. Sourdough also works wonderfully too. Buy loaves and slice off the tops and bottoms for a soft-yet-crisp exterior.

Look for cheeses that are gooey, but hold form when melted... Provolone, Gruyère, sharp cheddar, or mozzarella are just a few that work well. Oily cheese, such as Gorgonzola, can thin out, so add a bit of mozzarella to hold the sandwich together. Finely slice your salami and meats very finely so

PANINI

that they heat through in minimal cooking time. Roast or grill vegetables before assembling your panini—you can do this easily on your panini grill.

There's an easy way to take panini to another level. All you need is a tablespoon of sweet/sour flavor to offset the richness of the other ingredients. You can prepare additions such as roasted tomatoes, basil pesto, or caramelized onions from scratch using the recipes I've included here, but store-bought onion jam, jarred peperoncini (pickled sweet peppers), and oil-packed sun-blush tomatoes will also do the trick.

The cooking method is simplicity itself. Most of these recipes take just three minutes in total on a panini grill. Just lower the lid and let it cook. Having a panini grill is convenient if you enjoy making these sandwiches frequently, but it's not essential. There are many models, so research carefully and note that dishwasher-safe, removable grill plates make cleaning-up much easier! To make panini on a stovetop, heat a heavy skillet or ridged stovetop grill pan and press the oil-brushed sandwich down with a metal spatula for two minutes on each side.

There is one last compulsory step. Pour a glass of chilled white wine wine or crack open an ice-cold bottle of Italian beer and sit back and admire your grilled masterpieces. They didn't take long to make, did they? And I guarantee they won't last long on the plate!

egg, bacon, spinach, and sharp cheddar

This is a grown-up and far more sophisticated version of a bacon-and-egg sandwich. A handful of fresh spinach cuts through the richness of the bacon and cheese, adding a healthy touch.

Preheat a panini grill. Cut the top and bottom off the ciabatta so that it is about 1 inch thick. Save the crusts for another use. Slice open lengthwise and then cut in half. In a skillet, sauté the bacon until crisp. Remove the bacon from the skillet and discard most of the oil. Pour in the beaten egg, season well with salt and pepper, and let the eggs set like an omelet.

Divide the spinach between the two sandwiches. Top with the crispy bacon, then half of the omelet, and finish with the cheese. Brush both sides of the panini with a little oil and grill in the preheated panini grill for 2–3 minutes, or according to the manufacturer's instructions. The bread should be golden brown and the filling warmed through.

Serving suggestion: If you like a hot chili sauce, such as Tabasco, try sprinkling some over this panino to give it an extra flavor kick.

1 ciabatta loaf

6 slices of bacon

2 eggs, beaten

1 large handful baby spinach leaves

3 oz. sharp cheddar cheese, thinly sliced

sea salt and freshly ground black pepper

vegetable oil, for sautéing and brushing

Makes 2 panini

BREAKFAST PANINI

egg, mushroom, havarti, and dill

Danish Havarti is a mild yet tangy cheese that works particularly well with mushrooms. Sliced Emmental or Gouda would also be tasty in this panino.

1 ciabatta loaf

1½ cups sliced white button mushrooms

2 eggs, beaten

3 oz. Havarti cheese, thinly sliced

2 teaspoons chopped dill

sea salt and freshly ground black pepper

vegetable oil, for sautéing and brushing

Makes 2 panini

Preheat a panini grill. Cut the top and bottom off the ciabatta so that it is about 1 inch thick. Save the crusts for another use. Slice open lengthwise and cut in half.

Heat 1 tablespoon of oil in a skillet. Season the mushrooms with salt and pepper and gently sauté for 4 minutes. Remove the mushrooms from the skillet and set aside. Add another teaspoon of oil to the skillet, pour in the eggs and scramble them over low heat. Evenly distribute the cheese between the two sandwiches. Spoon on the scrambled egg, top with the mushrooms, and sprinkle with dill. Brush both sides of the panini with a little oil and grill in the preheated panini grill for 2–3 minutes, or according to the manufacturer's instructions. The bread should be golden brown and the filling warmed through.

Serving suggestion: Serve this satisfying panino with a generous dollop of gourmet tomato or mushroom ketchup.

smoked salmon, cream cheese, tomato, red onion, and caperberries

This classic combination of fillings, usually served in a bagel, becomes even more delicious when reinvented as a panino. A little peppery watercress or arugula makes a nice addition.

Preheat a panini grill. Cut the top and bottom off the ciabatta so that it is about 1 inch thick. Save the crusts for another use. Slice open lengthwise and cut in half.

Layer the fillings on the two sandwiches starting with the cream cheese, followed by the salmon, caperberries, red onion, tomato, and watercress, if using. Season well with salt and pepper. Brush both sides of the panini with a little oil and grill in the preheated panini grill for 2–3 minutes, or according to the manufacturer's instructions. The bread should be golden brown and the filling warmed through.

Serving suggestion: Sprinkle with some chopped fresh dill.

1 ciabatta loaf

4 tablespoons cream cheese

4 slices of smoked salmon

1 teaspoon small caperberries

2 teaspoons finely diced red onion

1 plum tomato, seeded and chopped

a small handful of watercress or arugula, optional

sea salt and freshly ground black pepper

vegetable oil, for brushing

Makes 2 panini

asparagus, fontina, and sun-blush tomatoes

Fontina is a creamy, nutty cheese from the mountains of Italy that melts like a dream.

Preheat a panini grill. Cut the top and bottom off the ciabatta loaf so that it is about 1 inch thick. Save the crusts for another use. Slice open lengthwise and cut in half.

Heat a little oil in a skillet. Add the asparagus, season with salt and pepper, and sauté for about 3 minutes. Divide the asparagus, cheese, and tomatoes between the two sandwiches. Brush both sides of the panini with a little oil and grill in the preheated panini grill for 2–3 minutes, or according to the manufacturer's instructions. The bread should be golden brown and the filling warmed through.

Serving suggestion: This is delicious drizzled with a little good-quality balsamic vinegar.

1 ciabatta loaf

10 asparagus spears

3½ oz. Fontina cheese, roughly grated

10 sun-blush tomatoes or Roasted Tomatoes (see page 60)

sea salt and freshly ground black pepper

olive oil, for sautéing and brushing

Makes 2 panini

bacon, potato, and red leicester, with tabasco sauce

Save your leftover baked or roasted potatoes to create this satisfying breakfast panino.

Preheat a panini press. Cut the top and bottom off the ciabatta so that it is about 1 inch thick. Save the crusts for another use. Slice open lengthwise and cut in half.

Add a little oil to a skillet and sauté the bacon until crisp. Remove from the skillet and drain on paper towels. Keep the skillet hot, add the potato slices and season them with salt and pepper. Sauté on both sides until crisp around the edges. Divide the bacon and potatoes between the two sandwiches. Add a dash of Tabasco and top with cheese. Brush both sides of the panini with a little oil and grill in the preheated panini grill for 3 minutes, or according to the manufacturer's instructions. The bread should be golden brown and the filling warmed through.

1 ciabatta loaf

6 slices of smoked bacon

1 large cooked potato, sliced

2 oz. Red Leicester or Monterey Jack, thinly sliced

2 teaspoons Tabasco sauce

sea salt and freshly ground black pepper

vegetable oil, for sautéing and brushing

Makes 2 panini

serrano ham, goat cheese, fig jam, and arugula

The sweet-and-sour fig jam suits the salty air-dried ham and creamy goat cheese perfectly. You could try other fruit jams such as quince or even a tomato chutney.

Preheat a panini grill. Cut the top and bottom off the ciabatta so that it is about 1 inch thick. Save the crusts for another use. Slice open lengthwise and then cut in half.

Spread the fig jam on both sandwiches and top with the ham, goat cheese, and arugula. Brush both sides of the panini with a little oil and grill in the preheated panini grill for 2–3 minutes, or according to the manufacturer's instructions. The bread should be golden brown and the filling warmed through.

Serving suggestion: Try this panino with the Smoky Paprika Mayonnaise on page 63 for dipping or, to make a more substantial meal, serve with a chicory and walnut salad simply dressed with vinaigrette.

1 ciabatta loaf
4 tablespoon good-quality fig jam
4 thin slices Serrano ham or prosciutto
3½ oz. firm goat cheese, crumbled
2 small handfuls of arugula
vegetable oil, for brushing

Makes 2 panini

PANINI with MEAT

spicy salami, provolone, artichoke, and peperoncini

1 ciabatta loaf

6 pieces of marinated artichoke

8 slices Napoli Piccante or other Italian salami

10 peperoncini (pickled hot peppers) or pickled peppadews, drained

2 tablespoons Basil Pesto (see page 61)

3 oz. Provolone cheese

vegetable oil, for brushing

Makes 2 panini

Provolone is the golden yellow, often pear-shaped, cheese seen hanging from a waxed string in Italian delis. It has a sharp, smoky taste and melts beautifully.

Preheat a panini grill. Cut the top and bottom off of the ciabatta so that it is about 1 inch thick. Save the crusts for another use. Slice open lengthwise and then cut in half.

Layer the fillings in the two sandwiches, starting with the artichoke, followed by the salami, peppers, and pesto, finishing with the cheese. Brush both sides of the panini with a little oil and grill in the preheated panini grill for 2–3 minutes, or according to the manufacturer's instructions. The bread should be golden brown and the filling warmed through.

Serving suggestion: Try the Lemon and Fennel Seed Mayonnaise on page 63 for dipping. Serve with a simple green side salad, dressed with balsamic vinegar.

chorizo, mozzarella, piquillos, and arugula

Spanish smoked paprika (pimentón) gives chorizo its characteristically rich, deep taste. Although you could use ordinary roasted peppers, do try to locate authentic piquillos as they are smoked in wood-burning ovens which gives them a flavor that is truly delectable.

Preheat a panini grill. Cut the top and bottom off the ciabatta so that it is about 1 inch high. Save the crusts for another use. Slice open lengthwise and then cut in half.

Layer the fillings in the two sandwiches, starting with the piquillos, followed by the chorizo and arugula, finishing with the cheese. Brush both sides of the panini with oil and grill in the preheated panini grill for 3 minutes, or according to the manufacturer's instructions. The bread should be golden brown and the filling warmed through.

Serving suggestion: Try making the Saffron Garlic Mayonnaise on page 63 and serve it on the side for dipping.

1 ciabatta loaf

4 whole piquillo peppers (or other small roasted red peppers), drained

12 slices chorizo sausage

2 handfuls of arugula

5 oz. (2 large balls) fresh buffalo mozzarella, drained and sliced

vegetable oil, for brushing

Makes 2 panini

turkey, gruyère, jalapeño, and mustard

1 ciabatta loaf

3 tablespoons grainy mustard

3½ oz. Gruyère or Emmental cheese, sliced or grated

2 tablespoons pickled jalapeño slices, drained

4 thick slices of turkey

vegetable oil, for brushing

Makes 2 panini

Put your leftover turkey meat to good use in this deliciously different panino. Jalapeño chilis are an excellent, unexpected partner here, but for a sweet rather than spicy sandwich, replace them with cranberry relish.

Preheat a panini grill. Cut the top and bottom off the ciabatta so that it is about 1 inch high. Save the crusts for another use. Slice open lengthwise and then cut in half.

Spread the mustard over the inside of each sandwich. Top with the cheese, follow with the jalapeños, and finish with the turkey. Brush both sides of the panini with oil and grill in the preheated panini press for 3 minutes, or according to the manufacturer's instructions. The bread should be golden brown and the filling warmed through.

Serving suggestion: Try serving this panino with the Mustard and Shallot Mayonnaise on page 63 for dipping, and with a simple tomato and red onion side salad.

bresaola, artichoke, parmesan, and arugula

Bresaola is a salt-cured, air-dried beef fillet from Lombardy in the north of Italy. It is sold at most deli counters these days but if you can't find it, thin slices of roast beef would work here too.

Preheat a panini grill. Cut the top and bottom off the ciabatta so that it is about 1 inch high. Save the crusts for another use. Slice open lengthwise and then cut in half.

Layer the fillings on the two sandwiches starting with the bresaola, then the artichokes, Parmesan, onion, and arugula, finishing with the cheese. Brush both sides of the panini with oil and grill in the preheated panini press for 3 minutes, or according to the manufacturer's instructions. The bread should be golden brown and the filling warmed through.

Serving suggestion: For extra flavor, drizzle this panino with a little good-quality balsamic vinegar.

1 ciabatta loaf

8 slices bresaola

6 pieces marinated artichoke

4 tablespoons grated Parmesan cheese

8 thinly sliced rings of red onion

2 handfuls of arugula

2½ oz. (1 ball) fresh buffalo mozzarella, drained and sliced

vegetable oil, for brushing

Makes 2 panini

chicken with gouda, red onion, and honey-mustard dressing

When melted, Dutch Gouda cheese becomes velvety and gooey, making it the ideal cheese for panini.

Preheat a panini grill. Cut the top and bottom off the ciabatta so that it is about 1 inch high. Save the crusts for another use. Slice open lengthwise and then cut in half.

Spread the honey-mustard dressing on the inside of both sandwiches. Slice the chicken into four pieces lengthwise. Layer the fillings in the two sandwiches starting with the chicken, followed by the onion and arugula, finishing with the cheese. Brush both sides of the panini with oil and grill in the preheated panini grill press for 3 minutes, or according to the manufacturer's instructions. The bread should be golden brown and the filling warmed through.

Serving suggestion: Serve this panino with extra honey-mustard dressing on the side for dipping.

1 ciabatta loaf

2 tablespoons store-bought honey-mustard dressing

1 cooked chicken breast

8 thinly sliced rings of red onion

2 handfuls of arugula

3 oz. Gouda cheese, sliced

vegetable oil, for brushing

Makes 2 panini

sausage, mozzarella, roasted bell peppers, and caramelized onions

Chunks of red bell pepper and deliciously spicy Italian sausage are married with oozing mozzarella in this unforgettable panino.

1 ciabatta loaf

3 Italian sausages, casings removed

4 tablespoons Caramelized Onions (see page 62)

4 tablespoons chopped roasted or grilled red bell peppers

5 oz. (2 balls) fresh buffalo mozzarella, drained and sliced

vegetable oil, for sautéing and brushing

Makes 2 panini

Preheat a panini grill. Cut the top and bottom off the ciabatta so that it is about 1 inch high. Save the crusts for another use. Slice open lengthwise and cut in half.

Heat a little oil in a skillet and sauté the sausage meat until crispy. Drain on paper towels and divide between the sandwiches. Top with onions, bell peppers, and then the cheese. Brush both sides of the panini with oil and grill in the preheated panini grill for 3 minutes, or according to the manufacturer's instructions. The bread should be golden brown and the filling warmed through.

pancetta, goat cheese, sun-blush tomato, and arugula

Use the firm-rinded goat cheese here as it melts more slowly than the soft variety.

1 ciabatta loaf

6 slices of pancetta or other unsmoked bacon

4 oz. firm goat cheese, crumbled or sliced

2 tablespoons chopped peperoncini (pickled hot peppers) or peppadews

2 handfuls of arugula

8 sun-blush tomatoes, drained of oil

vegetable oil, for sautéing and brushing

Makes 2 panini

Preheat a panini grill. Cut the top and bottom off the ciabatta so that it is about 1 inch high. Save the crusts for another use. Slice open lengthwise and cut in half.

Heat a little oil in a skillet and sauté the pancetta until crisp. Drain on paper towels. Layer the fillings in the two sandwiches, starting with the pancetta, then follow with the goat cheese, peperoncini, and arugula, finishing with the sun-blush tomatoes.

Brush both sides of the panini with oil and grill in the preheated panini grill for 3 minutes, or according to the manufacturer's instructions. The bread should be golden brown and the filling warmed through.

mortadella, provolone, giardiniera, and arugula

1 ciabatta loaf

4 thin slices of mortadella

4 tablespoons chopped Giardiniera (see page 62)

2 small handfuls of arugula

3 oz. Provolone cheese, thinly sliced

vegetable oil, for brushing

Makes 2 panini

Bologna, the gastronomic capital of Italy, is renowned for its Mortadella, a silky-textured mammoth salami. Salty Provolone cheese and giardiniera (little pickled vegetables) balance the flavors. You can buy giardiniera in small jars or try making your own.

Preheat a panini grill. Cut the top and bottom off the ciabatta so that it is about 1 inch high. Save the crusts for another use. Slice open lengthwise and then cut in half.

Layer the fillings in the two sandwiches, starting with the mortadella, and then adding the giardiniera and arugula, finishing with the cheese. Brush both sides of the panini with oil and grill in the preheated panini grill for 3 minutes, or according to the manufacturer's instructions. The bread should be golden brown and the filling warmed through.

Serving suggestion: Try serving this panino with a crisp green salad.

pepperoni, mozzarella, black olives, and pesto

This "pizzaiola panini" makes the ideal snack for lovers of authentic Italian pizza.

Preheat a panini grill. Cut the top and bottom off the ciabatta so that it is about 1 inch high. Save the crusts for another use. Slice open lengthways and cut in half.

Spread one half of each sandwich with tomato paste and the other side with pesto. Layer the fillings, starting with the pepperoni, followed by the olives and onion, finishing with the cheese. Brush both sides of the panini with oil and grill in the preheated panini grill for 3 minutes, or according to the manufacturer's instructions. The bread should be golden brown and the filling warmed through.

Serving suggestion: Serve with a radicchio and shaved fennel side salad.

1 ciabatta loaf

2 tablespoons tomato paste

2 tablespoons Basil Pesto (see page 61)

12 small thin slices of pepperoni sausage

10 pitted black olives, sliced

8 thinly sliced rings of red onion

5 oz. (2 large balls) fresh buffalo mozzarella, sliced

vegetable oil, for brushing

Makes 2 panini

tuna, celery, sharp cheddar, and sun-blush tomato on sourdough

Although you can of course use ciabatta, sourdough bread is a particularly good choice for this crunchy, easy-to-make sandwich.

4 slices sourdough bread

4 oz. (drained weight) canned tuna

1 tablespoons diced celery

1 tablespoons finely diced red onion

4 tablespoons Homemade Mayonnaise (see page 63)

6 sun-blush tomatoes, drained

2 oz. sharp Cheddar cheese, grated

sea salt and freshly ground black pepper

vegetable oil, for brushing

Makes 2 panini

Preheat a panini grill. Mix the tuna with the celery, onion, and mayonnaise and season with salt and pepper. Divide the tuna mixture between the two sandwiches, top with tomatoes and add the cheese.

Brush both sides of the panini with oil and grill in the preheated panini grill for 3 minutes, or according to the manufacturer's instructions. The bread should be golden brown and the filling warmed through.

pancetta, gorgonzola, apple, and arugula

Pancetta is delicious unsmoked Italian bacon. Its subtle taste and wafer-thin crispness ensure that it enhances but doesn't dominate the other ingredients.

1 ciabatta loaf
6 slices pancetta
2 teaspoons balsamic vinegar
½ a tart green apple, thinly sliced
a small handful of arugula
2½ oz. Gorgonzola cheese, crumbled
2½ oz. Taleggio or Fontina cheese, sliced
sea salt and freshly ground black pepper
vegetable oil, for sautéing and brushing

Makes 2 panini

Preheat a panini grill. Cut the top and bottom off the ciabatta so that it is about 1 inch high. Save the crusts for another use. Slice open lengthwise and then cut in half.

Add a little oil to a skillet and sauté the pancetta until crisp. Drain on paper towels. Drizzle both sandwiches with balsamic vinegar and season with salt and pepper. Layer the fillings in the sandwiches, starting with the pancetta, followed by the apple and arugula, and finishing with the cheeses. Brush both sides of the panini with oil and grill in the preheated panini grill for 3 minutes, or according to the manufacturer's instructions. The bread should be golden brown and the filling warmed through.

roast beef with caramelized onion, watercress, and horseradish

1 ciabatta loaf

2 tablespoons store-bought creamed horseradish

4 slices of roast beef

4 tablespoons Caramelized Onions (see page 62)

2 handfuls of watercress

2 oz. Gruyère cheese, sliced

vegetable oil, for brushing

Makes 2 panini

This unusual panino has the deliciously mustardy addition of creamed horseradish, which is the natural partner to beef.

Preheat a panini grill. Cut the top and bottom off the ciabatta so that it is about 1 inch high. Save the crusts for another use. Slice open lengthwise and cut in half.

Spread the creamed horseradish on the inside of both sandwiches. Layer the fillings, starting with the beef, then the onions and watercress and finish with the cheese. Brush both sides of the panini with oil and grill in the preheated panini grill for 3 minutes, or according to the manufacturer's instructions. The bread should be golden brown and the filling warmed through.

Serving suggestion: Serve this panino with a little extra creamed horseradish if you like things hot.

prosciutto, balsamic fig, fontina, and arugula

Fontina works beautifully with figs and prosciutto but you could also use mozzarella.

1 ciabatta loaf
4 slices prosciutto
2–3 ripe figs, sliced
2 teaspoons balsamic vinegar
2 handfuls of arugula
2½ oz. Fontina cheese
sea salt and freshly ground black pepper
vegetable oil, for brushing

Makes 2 panini

Preheat a panini grill. Cut the top and bottom off the ciabatta so that it is about 1 inch high. Save the crusts for another use. Slice open lengthwise and then cut in half.

Divide the prosciutto between the two sandwiches. Top with fig slices, sprinkle with vinegar, and season to taste with salt and pepper. Add the arugula and then the cheese. Brush both sides of the panini with oil and grill in the preheated panini grill for 3 minutes, or according to the manufacturer's instructions. The bread should be golden brown and the filling warmed through.

salami, roasted fennel, fontina, and caperberries

Other pickled condiments would be equally good here in place of the caperberries.

1 ciabatta loaf

8 slices Italian salami

4 slices of Roasted Fennel, roughly chopped (see page 60)

8 thinly sliced rings of red onion

2 teaspoons small caperberries

2½ oz. Fontina cheese, sliced or grated

vegetable oil, for brushing

Makes 2 panini

Preheat a panini grill. Cut the top and bottom off the ciabatta so that it is about 1 inch high. Save the crusts for another use. Slice open lengthwise and then cut in half.

Layer the salami, fennel, onion, caperberries, and then cheese in both sandwiches. Brush both sides of the panini with oil and grill in the preheated panini grill for 3 minutes, or according to the manufacturer's instructions. The bread should be golden brown and the filling warmed through.

Serving suggestion: Try this panino with the Lemon and Fennel Seed Mayonnaise on page 63 for dipping.

chicken, scamorza, roasted tomato, and watercress

Scamorza is smoked mozzarella cheese. It has a more pronounced flavor and firmer texture than the fresh variety. Sun-blush tomatoes can be subsituted for the roasted tomatoes if you are short on time.

Preheat a panini grill. Cut the top and bottom off the ciabatta so that it is about 1 inch high. Save the crusts for another use. Slice open lengthwise and then cut in half.

Slice the chicken into 4 pieces lengthwise. Layer two slices in each sandwich and follow with the tomatoes, watercress, and then the cheese. Brush both sides of the panini with oil and grill in the preheated panini grill for 3 minutes, or according to the manufacturer's instructions. The bread should be golden brown and the filling warmed through.

Serving suggestion: Try the Fresh Herb Mayonnaise on page 63 for dipping or add a drizzle of balsamic vinegar.

1 ciabatta loaf

1 cooked chicken breast

4 slices Roasted Tomatoes (see page 60)

2 handfuls of watercress

3 oz. Scamorza cheese, thinly sliced

vegetable oil, for brushing

Makes 2 panini

garlic greens with provolone

Any type of green, including kale or swiss chard, can be used in this recipe. It's important to blanch even tender greens before searing in garlic, as this removes any bitterness. Ricotta or Gorgonzola would work nicely in place of the Provolone.

Preheat a panini grill. Cut the top and bottom off the ciabatta so that it is about 1 inch thick. Save the crusts for another use. Slice open lengthwise and cut in half.

Blanch the greens in salted water for 2 minutes and then drain. In a skillet, heat the olive oil. Add the garlic and pepper flakes. Drop the greens in and season with salt and pepper. Toss for a minute and remove from the heat. Divide the greens between the two sandwiches and top with the cheese. Brush both sides of the panini with a little oil and grill in the preheated panini grill for 2–3 minutes, or according to the manufacturer's instructions. The bread should be golden brown and the filling warmed through.

Serving suggestion: Serve this panini with a red and yellow tomato salad with sliced scallions.

1 ciabatta loaf

2 cups spring greens, roughly chopped

2 tablespoons olive oil

1 garlic clove

a pinch of dried hot pepper flakes

2½ oz. Provolone cheese

sea salt and freshly ground black pepper

vegetable oil, for brushing

Makes 2 panini

VEGETABLE PANINI

gruyère, sharp cheddar, and scallions on sourdough

This is no ordinary grilled cheese sandwich. The mixture of Swiss Gruyère and sharp Cheddar with scallions is pure heaven.

4 slices sourdough bread

2 oz. Gruyère cheese, grated

2 oz. sharp Cheddar cheese, grated

2 scallions, thinly sliced

sea salt and freshly ground black pepper

vegetable oil, for brushing

Makes 2 panini

Preheat a panini grill. Lay the slices of bread out. Divide the cheeses between the two sandwiches, add the scallions, and season with salt and pepper. Put the tops on. Brush both sides of the panini with a little oil and grill in the preheated panini grill for 2–3 minutes, or according to the manufacturer's instructions. The bread should be golden brown and the filling warmed through.

Serving suggestion: Try this panino with a dollop of grainy mustard on the side for dipping and a baby spinach leaf salad.

grilled zucchini, red onion, goat cheese, and mint

Zucchini are completely transformed by grilling as their flavor intensifies and becomes sweeter.

Preheat a panini grill. Cut the top and bottom off the ciabatta so that it is about 1 inch thick. Save the crusts for another use. Slice open lengthwise and then cut in half.

Brush the zucchini with a little oil and season with salt and pepper. Grill them for 1–2 minutes in the preheated panini grill or a ridged stovetop grill pan. Divide the zucchini between the two sandwiches. Top with the onions, mint, and arugula, finishing with the cheese. Brush both sides of the panini with a little oil and toast in the preheated panini press for 2–3 minutes, or according to the manufacturer's instructions. The bread should be golden brown and the filling warmed through.

Serving suggestion: Try this panino with some slices of fresh radish on the side and a drizzle of balsamic vinegar.

1 ciabatta loaf

2 small zucchini, cut lengthwise into slices ¼ inch thick

8 thinly sliced rings of red onion

1 tablespoon chopped mint

2 handfuls of arugula

3½ oz. firm goat cheese, crumbled

sea salt and freshly ground black pepper

olive oil, for brushing

Makes 2 panini

roasted fennel, tomato, fontina, and pesto

If you don't have time to make up a batch of roasted fennel and tomatoes, raid your local market's deli counter for Italian-style substitutes such as grilled zucchini or eggplant, or marinated "antipasti-style" mushrooms.

1 ciabatta loaf

2 tablespoons Basil Pesto (see page 61)

6 Roasted Tomatoes (see page 60)

4 slices Roasted Fennel, roughly chopped (see page 60)

3 oz. Fontina or mozzarella cheese

vegetable oil, for brushing

Makes 2 panini

Preheat a panini grill. Cut the top and bottom off the ciabatta so that it is about 1 inch thick. Save the crusts for another use. Slice open lengthwise and cut in half.

Spread the pesto on the inside of both sandwiches. Place 3 tomatoes and 2 slices of fennel on each. Top with equal amounts of cheese. Brush both sides of the panini with a little oil and grill in the preheated panini grill for 2–3 minutes, or according to the manufacturer's instructions. The bread should be golden brown and the filling warmed through.

Serving suggestion: Try this panino with a small bowl of peperoncini (pickled hot peppers), the Giardiniera (pickled vegetables) on page 62 or a simple cherry tomato and fresh basil salad.

portobello mushrooms with taleggio and pesto

Who needs meat when you have Portobello mushrooms? The texture of these large mushrooms is chewy, and they're surprisingly filling, particularly when smothered with tangy Taleggio cheese.

1 ciabatta loaf

2 tablespoons Basil Pesto (see page 61)

4 large Portobello mushrooms, stems removed

2 tablespoons balsamic vinegar

3½ oz. Taleggio cheese

sea salt and freshly ground black pepper

olive oil, for brushing

Makes 2 panini

Preheat a panini grill. Cut the top and bottom off the ciabatta so that it is about 1 inch thick. Save the crusts for another use. Slice open lengthwise and then cut in half.

Spread the pesto on the inside of each. Brush the mushrooms with oil and drizzle with balsamic vinegar. Season with salt and pepper and grill for 1–2 minutes in the preheated panini press or a ridged stovetop grill pan. Place a mushroom in each sandwich and top with the cheese. Brush both sides of the panini with a little oil and grill in the preheated panini grill for 2–3 minutes, or according to the manufacturer's instructions. The bread should be golden brown and the filling warmed through.

Serving suggestion: Try this panino with the Saffron Garlic Mayonnaise on page 63.

grilled eggplant, red onion, ricotta, and sun-blush tomato pesto

There is a marked difference between supermarket ricotta and what you will find in an Italian store. The latter is fresh, creamy and glorious with grilled eggplant.

Preheat a panini grill. Cut the top and bottom off the ciabatta so that it is about 1 inch thick. Save the crusts for another use. Slice open lengthwise and then cut in half.

Spread the pesto on the inside of both the sandwiches. Brush the eggplant with some olive oil and balsamic vinegar and season with salt and pepper. Grill the slices for 1–2 minutes in the preheated panini grill or a ridged stovetop grill pan. Roughly chop them and divide between the sandwiches. Top with the basil and onions and finish with the ricotta. Brush both sides of the panini with a little oil and grill in the preheated panini grill for 2 minutes, or according to the manufacturer's instructions. The bread should be golden brown and the filling warmed through.

Serving suggestion: Try this with a handful of corn salad on the side.

1 ciabatta loaf

2 tablespoons Sun-blush Tomato Pesto (see page 61)

1 medium eggplant, cut into slices ¼ inch thick

2 tablespoons balsamic vinegar

2 tablespoons chopped fresh basil

8 thinly sliced rings of red onion

2½ oz. ricotta "fresca" cheese

sea salt and freshly ground black pepper

olive oil, for brushing

Makes 2 panini

caramelized onions, gorgonzola, rosemary, and watercress

Spicy watercress is ideal for panini. Like arugula, and unlike most other salad greens, it isn't too too watery and provides the perfect peppery punch.

1 ciabatta loaf
4 tablespoons Caramelized Onions (see page 62)
1 teaspoon finely chopped fresh rosemary
2 handfuls of watercress
1½ oz. Gorgonzola cheese, sliced
1½ oz. Fontina or mozzarella cheese, sliced
vegetable oil, for brushing

Makes 2 panini

Preheat a panini grill. Cut the top and bottom off the ciabatta so that it is about 1 inch thick. Save the crusts for another use. Slice open lengthwise and cut in half.

Place the onions in both the sandwiches and sprinkle with rosemary. Top with watercress and then finish with the cheeses. Brush both sides of the panini with a little oil and grill in the preheated panini grill for 2–3 minutes, or according to the manufacturer's instructions. The bread should be golden brown and the filling warmed through.

mozzarella, anchovy, lemon, and red onion

This bold Sicilian trio of anchovy, garlic, and lemon is just the right accent for creamy mozzarella.

1 ciabatta loaf
2 tablespoons olive oil
2 garlic cloves, sliced
1 anchovy fillet, rinsed of oil
4 tablespoons chopped parsley
finely grated peel of 1 lemon
5 oz. (2 large balls) fresh buffalo mozzarella, sliced
4 tablespoons Caramelized Onions (see page 62)
vegetable oil, for brushing

Makes 2 panini

Preheat a panini grill. Cut the top and bottom off the ciabatta so that it is about 1 inch thick. Save the crusts for another use. Slice open lengthwise and then cut in half.

Heat the olive oil in a small skillet. Add the garlic and anchovy. Cook until the garlic is golden and the anchovy starts to break up. Remove from the heat and add the parsley and lemon zest. Spread the mixture over the inside of both sandwiches.

Top with the cheese and caramelized onions. Brush both sides of the panini with a little oil and grill in the preheated panini grill for 2–3 minutes, or according to the manufacturer's instructions. The bread should be golden brown and the filling warmed through.

Serving suggestion: Serve this panino with a crisp raddichio salad.

kirsch-soaked cherries and nectarine, with cream cheese and almonds

Cherries are delicious here but you can try any other fruit that's in season at the same time, such as strawberries.

Preheat a panini grill. Put the cherries and nectarine slices in a large bowl, add the kirsch and toss gently. Spread the cream cheese on two of the slices of brioche. Press the cherries and nectarines on top and then sprinkle with the almonds and sugar. Top with the other two pieces of bread and press them together.

Brush both sides of the panini with a little oil and toast in the preheated panini press for 2 minutes, or according to the manufacturer's instructions. The bread should be golden brown and the filling warmed through.

4 thick slices brioche bread

12 fresh cherries, pitted

1 nectarine, pitted and thinly sliced

1 tablespoon kirsch

4 tablespoons cream cheese

2 tablespoons slivered almonds, lightly toasted

1 tablespoon Demerara sugar

vegetable oil, for brushing

Makes 2 panini

SWEET PANINI

raspberry and mascarpone on brioche

Rethink dessert with this simple but stellar panini. Use white bread with the crusts removed if you can't find brioche.

4 thick slices brioche bread
4 tablespoons mascarpone
2 handfuls of raspberries
2 teaspoons Demerara sugar
vegetable oil, for brushing

Spread two slices of the bread with the mascarpone cheese. Place the raspberries on top and sprinkle with the sugar. Top both sandwiches with the second slice. Brush both sides of the panini with a little oil and grill in the preheated panini grill for 2 minutes, or according to the manufacturer's instructions. The bread should be golden brown and the filling warmed through.

Serving suggestion: Alternatively, try this panini with thin slices of fresh strawberries instead of the raspberries.

nutella and bananas on brioche

Children (and adults) around the world are grateful for one of Italy's biggest exports—Nutella. This luxurious chocolate spread made with hazelnuts and chocolate, is marvelous just scooped up and devoured by the spoonful. But when warmed up between two pieces of brioche with some banana it becomes something sublime!

Preheat a panini grill. Spread 2 slices of the brioche with the Nutella. Place the banana slices on top. Close the sandwiches with the second slice of brioche. Brush both sides of the panini with a little oil and grill in the preheated panini grill for 2 minutes, or according to the manufacturer's instructions. The bread should be golden brown and the filling warmed through.

Serving suggestion: As an alternative, try replacing the Nutella with a good-quality peanut butter.

4 thick slices brioche bread

4 tablespoons Nutella or other chocolate-hazelnut spread

1 small banana, thinly sliced

vegetable oil, for brushing

CONDIMENTI

roasted tomatoes

These are wonderful in just about any recipe, from pasta to pizza.

6 large Italian plum tomatoes
2 garlic cloves, thickly sliced
1 teaspoon sea salt
½ teaspoon cracked black pepper
2 tablespoons olive oil
1 tablespoon balsamic vinegar

Makes 12 halves

Preheat oven to 325°F. Slice the tomatoes in half lengthwise. Place in a large roasting pan lined with foil. Sprinkle the garlic, salt, and pepper over and drizzle with olive oil. Bake in the preheated oven for 45 minutes. Remove, drizzle with vinegar, and let sit for 10 minutes. When cool, pack into an airtight container. Once sealed, the tomatoes will keep in the fridge for up to 1 week.

roasted fennel

Liquorice-flavored fennel becomes very sweet when roasted. A little boiling water in the pan keeps the flesh soft while the edges crisp up and caramelize.

4 large fennel bulbs
2 garlic cloves, thickly sliced
1 teaspoon sea salt
½ teaspoon cracked black pepper
2 tablespoons olive oil
1 tablespoon balsamic vinegar

Makes 8–10 slices

Preheat oven to 325°F. Cut the fennel in half lengthwise and cut the core out. Slice the pieces about ½ inch thick and place in a large roasting pan lined with foil. Sprinkle the garlic, salt, and pepper over and drizzle with olive oil. Put the fennel in the preheated oven to roast for 1 hour. About 15 minutes into the cooking time pour ½ cup of boiling water into the pan. When cooked, drizzle with the vinegar. Once cool, pack in an airtight container. When sealed the fennel will keep in the fridge for up to 1 week.

basil pesto

Jarred pesto just doesn't have the same heady aroma as homemade. If you buy it then look for brands that are made with 100 percent olive oil.

1 large garlic clove, crushed
3½ oz. pine nuts, toasted
2 bunches fresh basil,
stems removed
⅔ cup extra virgin olive oil
3½ oz. Parmesan cheese, finely grated
sea salt

Makes 1½ cups

Place the garlic, pine nuts, and basil in a food processor. Keep the motor running and slowly pour in the olive oil. Scrape the mixture into a bowl and stir in the Parmesan and a small pinch of salt.

Pour the pesto into an airtight container. Once sealed the pesto will keep in the fridge for up to 10 days.

sun-blush tomato pesto

Sun-blush tomatoes are a hybrid between sun-dried and oven-roasted. More subtle in taste, they are softer and juicier than sun-dried.

5½ oz. sun-blush tomatoes, drained
3½ oz. pine nuts, toasted
1 garlic clove
2 oz. Parmesan cheese, grated
1 teaspoon dried hot pepper flakes
½ cup extra virgin olive oil
sea salt and freshly ground black pepper

Makes 2 cups

In a food processor combine the tomatoes, pine nuts, garlic, Parmesan, and pepper flakes. Keep the motor running and slowly pour in the olive oil. Add salt and pepper to taste. Spoon the pesto into an airtight container. Once sealed the pesto will keep in the fridge for up to 1 week.

caramelized onions

You can buy jars of caramelized onion jam but homemade are much tastier.

3 tablespoons olive oil
2 large onions, thinly sliced
1 tablespoon red wine vinegar
1 teaspoon superfine sugar
1 teaspoon sea salt
½ teaspoon cracked black pepper

Makes 1½ cups

Heat the oil in a large skillet. Add the onions, salt, and pepper and sauté for 3 minutes over high heat. Turn the heat down to medium/low and sauté for 20 minutes more. Add the vinegar and sugar and cook for 5 more minutes. Remove from the heat. When cool, spoon into an airtight container. Refrigerate for up to 1 week.

giardiniera

Do try these delicious little pickles.

½ a small head cauliflower
1 red bell pepper, cored and seeded
2 medium carrots
2 celery stalks, sliced
½ cup Sicilian green olives, pitted
¼ cup peperoncini (pickled hot peppers)

Pickling liquid:
1¼ cups white wine vinegar
1½ cups water
⅓ cup sugar
2½ tablespoons sea salt
a pinch of hot pepper flakes
½ teaspoon yellow mustard seeds

Makes 3 cups

Chop all of the vegetables into ½ inch pieces. Pour the pickling ingredients into a saucepan and heat until the sugar is dissolved. Let cool. Bring a large saucepan of salted water to a boil. Blanch all the vegetables (except for the olives and peperoncini) individually. Refresh them in a bowl of ice water and drain on paper towels. Add to the pickling liquid. Weight the pickles down with a plate to keep them submerged and refrigerate, covered, for 24 hours before using. The pickles will keep in the fridge for up to 2 weeks.

homemade mayonnaise

Serve your panini with this delicious homemade mayonnaise on the side.

1 tablespoon Dijon mustard
½ teaspoon sea salt
½ teaspoon white pepper
2 egg yolks, at room temperature
¾ cup grapeseed or sunflower oil
3 tablespoons extra virgin olive oil
1 tablespoon freshly squeezed lemon juice
1 teaspoon superfine sugar

Makes 2 cups

In a food processor pulse the mustard, salt, and pepper and egg yolks. With the motor running, slowly drizzle in the oils until they are incorporated. Add the lemon juice and sugar and pulse again. Spoon into an airtight container. Refrigerate for up to 4 days.

Variations

Simply stir these extra ingredients into the freshly prepared mayonnaise:

Saffron garlic—Add 1 teaspoon crushed saffron threads (soaked in 1 tablespoon hot water) and 1 crushed garlic clove.

Caperberry, chive, and onion—Add 1 tablespoon each of chopped caperberries, chives, and caramelized onion.

Fresh herb—Add 3 tablespoons mixed fresh chopped herbs such as tarragon, parsley, basil, cilantro, chives, or dill.

Orange, olive, and parsley—Add 1 tablespoon finely grated orange peel, 1 tablespoon chopped black olives, and 2 tablespoons chopped parsley.

Smoky paprika—Add 1 tablespoon sweet Spanish paprika (*pimentón dulce*), 1 crushed garlic clove, and 1 teaspoon finely grated lemon peel.

Lemon and fennel seed—Add the finely grated peel of 1 lemon, 1 tablespoon freshly squeezed lemon juice, 1 teaspoon ground fennel seeds, and 1 tablespoon chopped parsley.

Mustard and shallot—Add 2 tablespoons grainy mustard, 1 tablespoon Dijon mustard, and 1 tablespoon finely chopped shallot.

index

conversion chart

Weights and measures have been rounded up or down slightly to make measuring easier.

American	Metric	Imperial
6 tbsp	85 g	3 oz
7 tbsp	100 g	3½ oz
1 stick	115 g	4 oz

Volume equivalents:

American	Metric	Imperial
1 teaspoon	5 ml	
1 tablespoon	15 ml	
¼ cup	60 ml	2 fl oz
⅓ cup	75 ml	2½ fl oz
½ cup	125 ml	4 fl oz
⅔ cup	150 ml	5 fl oz (¼ pint)
¾ cup	175 ml	6 fl oz
1 cup	250 ml	8 fl oz

Weight equivalents:

Imperial	Metric
1 oz	30 g
2 oz	55 g
3 oz	85 g
3½ oz	100 g
4 oz	115 g
6 oz	175 g
8 oz (½ lb)	225 g
9 oz	250 g
10 oz	280 g
12 oz	350 g
13 oz	375 g
14 oz	400 g
15 oz	425 g
16 oz (1 lb)	450 g

Measurements:

Inches	cm
¼ inch	5 mm
½ inch	1 cm
1 inch	2.5 cm
2 inches	5 cm
3 inches	7 cm
4 inches	10 cm
5 inches	12 cm
6 inches	15 cm
7 inches	18 cm
8 inches	20 cm
9 inches	23 cm
10 inches	25 cm
11 inches	28 cm
12 inches	30 cm

Oven temperatures:

120°C	(250°F)	Gas ½
140°C	(275°F)	Gas 1
150°C	(300°F)	Gas 2
170°C	(325°F)	Gas 3
180°C	(350°F)	Gas 4
190°C	(375°F)	Gas 5
200°C	(400°F)	Gas 6